Getting THE Most FROM God

(but not how you
might think!)

John Revell

ISBN 978-0-9754120-1-5

Published by Ginosko Publishing, Inc.
Nashville, Tennessee

Cover and book design by Rick Boyd

Table of Contents

Introduction

It seems like everyone wants to hit the heavenly lottery. Millions of people around the world are fueling greedy tel-evangelists who promise them perfect health and incredible wealth if they will just "have enough faith." Millions of books have been sold offering secret formulas for tapping into the riches of heaven. And some very unusual and unprincipled preachers are getting filthy rich off the ignorance, desperation, and greed of those who are willing to be sucked in by these distortions and lies.

Don't get me wrong, God *truly* wants His children to experience all of His richest blessings. However, God did not craft those blessings to gratify the desires of the greedy; nor does He lavish them on those who are always approaching Him with their hands out. In fact, the Bible indicates that He doesn't care much for that kind of attitude.

At the same time, the Bible is clear that God *rewards those who earnestly seek him* (Heb. 11:6 NIV). Throughout the Bible we find that God offers incredible rewards—but they are conditional.

In this book, we'll look at two passages from the Psalms and two passages from the Gospels that touch on some of these rewards. There we'll find that when we meet the necessary conditions, God promises to give us several things, including:

- the desires of our hearts;
- joys and pleasures;
- absolute and ultimate victory over Satan; and even
- extended family, houses, and land.

But I'll let you know right up front—none of these are promised as a direct result of pursuing them—they come as the result of other actions and mindsets that are addressed in each passage. It would be difficult for you to find examples in the Bible where God granted these specific blessings as a result of someone chasing after them—His blessings were usually given when a person was focused on other priorities. In fact, here's the monumental irony from this study: God gives the greatest rewards to those who are not specifically chasing after them.

God gives the greatest rewards to those who are not specifically chasing after them.

Also, you should know from the outset that the fulfillment of these promises may not look exactly like what you might have expected—but they will likely be far greater than you could have ever imagined.

You may have picked up this book because you've heard television evangelists claim that God wants you to be healthy and wealthy. You need to understand that they are not telling you the truth—and many, perhaps even most, of those who make this claim have ulterior motives—they want you to send them money.

I have the joy and pleasure of leading a discipleship

group with some incredible high-school and college young men. Three of them—Stephen, Justin, and my son Philip—decided to have some fun with me by giving my name and address to one of these crack-pot, faux evangelists. Shortly after, I received a letter from him containing a vial of "miracle spring water." He indicated that if I drank the spring water (and sent him at least $30) God would deliver me from the crushing financial and physical bondage I was under (which I didn't realize I was experiencing!). He continued to send letters, promising untold wealth and physical blessings if I would merely follow his (bizarre) instructions—and send him money. The last letter included a vial of "Miracle Green Prosperity Oil." I was instructed to put a drop under my dining room chair, another on the mat outside my front door, and one beside my bed—if I did (and sent him $33), this oil would protect me from the amassing spiritual forces of darkness that he knew to be threatening me, and I would become incredibly wealthy.

Of course, not every TV or radio ministry is like this—there really are some excellent, honorable ministers and ministries on the air waves. But this man had the gall to announce that all this nonsense was coming from God Himself!

This book is not about that. If that's what you were looking for, at first you may be disappointed at what you find here. But if you read the whole book, and if you take the necessary actions explained in the passages, what you encounter will exceed your wildest dreams.

You may have bought this book merely out of curiosity. If so, read on. You will be blown away by what God's Word has to say to you.

You may be reading this book as a skeptic, thinking this is just another scam. I promise you, I am not asking for any money (aside from the cost of the book, of course). I also promise that what you find here will be absolutely true to the Word of God, with no enhancements, embellishments, or unique insights. I have not received additional special revelation for this book—I have not received any visions about such things—I am merely pointing out what God has already revealed in His Word. It is there for all to see without any special insights from anyone else.

So, are you willing to do whatever it takes to reach

that point where you are overwhelmed by the "glorious riches of His inheritance in the saints?"

Are you ready to become the person God truly blesses?

Maybe you are—maybe not.

Read on to find out.

Notes

Chapter One

The Desires of Your Heart

THE FIRST PROMISE WE WILL CONSIDER IS found in Psalm 37:4. Here it is:

Delight yourself in the LORD, and he will give you the desires of your heart (ESV).

Go back and read the passage again. The promise is simple, isn't it? God offers us the desires of our hearts! It's right there in God's Word, and there is no disputing it.

But what does that mean?

DESIRES

The thought of getting the desires of our hearts sounds pretty good, doesn't it? Stop and think: What are the deepest desires of your heart right now?

Dark Desires of the Heart

Now honestly, all of us at some point, deep down in the darkest parts of our hearts, have craved and longed for things that we know are not appropriate. We don't need anyone to tell us they're wrong, we know already—things like:

Sensual Lusts—a truly dark desire of the heart. The multi-billion-dollar porn industry in our nation exists because of this craving. Millions of men have become slaves to their ravenous appetites for such gratifications. Prime time television has become saturated with sexual material because this dark desire is so prominent in our homes.

Alcohol and illegal drug sales thrive in our nation because people are craving the physical pleasures associated with them.

Obesity is virtually an epidemic in our society because of the pleasure associated with eating. Premature deaths related to obesity are second only to tobacco related deaths in our nation, and it is directly linked to the number one killer in our nation—heart disease. Weight loss programs are thriving in our land because people have such a hard time saying "no" to their desires.

Greed—longing to be "filthy" rich. It is so easy to become greedy and want lots of money, isn't it? That's why the lottery is so successful in so many states. The people buying those lottery tickets aren't doing it because they just really want to help the educational system in their states—no, they're slapping money down on the convenience store counters to buy those tickets because they want to hit it big!

The casinos that are popping up in so many states aren't there merely as a recreational option. The people who walk in there with a little cash in their pockets hope to walk out with a whole lot more.

Every time someone puts a quarter in a slot machine, he/she hopes the next yank on that "one armed bandit" will light up lights, set off bells and alarms, and send buckets of coins spewing out of its mouth.

And everyone who fills out those forms for the *Publisher's Clearinghouse Sweepstakes* has the same dream—seeing that van pull up in front of their house carrying camera crews and people in nice suits who get out and walk up to the front door with a check for $10 million—with your name on it.

Greed is a powerful force in our nation—otherwise we wouldn't have so many lawyers specializing in civil suits that seek millions of dollars in "damages" for ridiculous claims.

Recognition and Praise—a third dark desire of the heart; that longing for esteem from friends, co-workers, and even family members. That's why there are jokes about staying one step ahead of the neighbors. That's why when some people introduce themselves they are anxious to reveal their vocation (especially if it is a high-paying or prestigious position). That's why some people buy the cars they do. That's why some people drop names. Face it: we like to be well thought of, to be popular and respected, and it is so easy to fall into this trap of seeking prominence and prestige.

Jesus' disciple, the apostle John, called these *the lust of the flesh and the lust of the eyes and the boastful pride of life* (1 John 2:16 NASB). John also identified these desires as worldly and an inappropriate focus for those who follow Christ. The Lord never promised to satisfy these self-seeking and self-serving desires. In fact, when we focus on these, when we set our hearts on any of them, we will never be satisfied. No matter how much we receive in any of these three areas—it will never be enough.

Appropriate Longings

Not all of our desires are so rooted in self-centeredness. You've probably longed for things that are more appropriate, things such as:

Deep Internal Peace—reaching the point where you are not anxious about all that is going on around you. You may have heard Jewish friends use the phrase "*shalom.*" That's a Hebrew word that means more than just peace; it also carries the idea of wholeness, completeness, and wellness. We live in a world of turmoil, struggle, anxiety, confusion, and danger. Our homes, schools, offices, nation, and world seem to be in upheaval. It is entirely understandable that we would long for deep inner peace in the midst of all this chaos.

Relational Harmony—with your roommate or spouse, with the kids, with the parents, with the neighbors, with the boss or co-workers. There seems to be so much conflict swirling around us. People seem like they are always mad, ready to bite each other's head off about something. Shows like *SuperNanny* and *Dr. Phil* wouldn't be so popular if they were not striking a chord with viewers. Wouldn't it be nice for there to be a sense of accord in the family or with co-workers? It's completely appropriate to long for everyone to "just get along" with each other.

Financial Stability—so that you're not worried about being able to pay the bills, or having money for the kids' education, or money to retire with. It's not greedy to long for your finances to be in order—to be able to cover all of your financial responsibilities, to plan for the future, and even to be able to give some to those in need.

Joy—to just be truly and deeply happy for a while. This isn't just laughter—we can get that from some TV shows. The problem comes when the show is over and the laughter stops. I'm talking about the kind of joy when you find yourself humming or whistling a tune as you walk, or smiling when you don't even realize it. This is a joy so deep that it affects how you see everything around you. It makes you ready to celebrate all the good things happening in the lives of those around you, rather than focusing on all the bad.

Love—to have someone care for you, not for what you can give back, but just for who you are. There is nothing wrong with longing for a relationship that is giving, forgiving, caring, nurturing, tender, compassionate, and selfless.

Wouldn't it be nice to have these as a part of everyday life? Desiring such things is understandable and appropriate, but can they ever be realized? Some people might conclude that having all of these—or even several of these—at the same time is unrealistic, that it is "pie in the sky by and by."

But go back to the passage. It says that God offers to give us the desires of our heart—HOWEVER, look at the condition—the offer is good only IF we *delight* ourselves in Him.

So what does that mean?

DELIGHT

Stop and think—what are the things you delight in most?

When I teach this in a Bible study format, I will ask for a list of things that guys most often take delight in. Here is what typically is listed:

- sports
- cars
- girls (some of the girls have suggested that this is where they really fall in order of priority)
- working out
- golf
- hunting
- fishing
- bowling
- watching TV
- eating

When I ask the girls what they delight in, they typically say:

- shopping
- talking
- guys (and the guys have responded that they fall in this order or priority)
- working out
- tennis
- golf

- being with girlfriends
- going out to eat
- watching certain TV shows

When you look closely at each of these lists, you realize that there must be a serious commitment of time for there to be a serious level of delight. None of the activities listed above are truly enjoyed without a significant investment of time—our weekly schedules typically indicate where our greatest delights lie.

Okay, I'm going to be a little transparent here (which is hard for us guys to do). Honestly, I take incredible delight in my wife and two sons. Some of the greatest joys in my life are directly linked to my relationship with them. And you know what? It has taken time—time being together and having fun with them, time praying for and with them, and time working through the various difficulties of life.

Both of the boys are grown now, and the times we share together today are more precious than ever. But that didn't start when they graduated from high school. From the earliest days of childhood I set aside at least two nights a week to be with them. When they were younger, we read countless books together. When they were older, we would go play racquetball together, or just drive around and hang out. And today, the time we spend together is so rich and rewarding to me—but it would not be that way without having invested so much time together earlier.

My wife, Debbie, is the most precious person in my life. The times of greatest and deepest delight in my life are linked to her and second only to my time spent directly with the Lord. As I write, I reflect back on twenty-eight years of being married to her. I cannot describe the delight—the sheer joy—that I take in her. But this is not merely because we exchanged wedding vows and rings almost three decades ago. We have invested a lot of time in our relationship.

To delight in the Lord requires a significant investment of time with Him.

Now, if twenty-eight years ago I announced to Debbie that I loved her so much I would set aside one hour each weekend to be together, and that I might be able to squeeze in five minutes a day with her from time to time (because I know I'm supposed to), but that the rest of my time was mine to pursue my own hobbies and interests, I don't think our relationship would be so blessed. In fact, I think it would have gotten rather chilly early on.

You see the point. To delight in the Lord requires a significant investment of time with Him. And the way we spend time with Him is by spending time in His Word and in prayer.

God's Word

Psalm 119 is an absolutely amazing chapter—not only is it the longest chapter of the Bible, it all focuses on God's Word. I'd like to look at just a few verses from this passage that reflect the mindset of a person who is truly delighting in the Lord.

My soul is consumed with longing for your laws at all times (Ps. 119:20 NIV).

That's amazing—to be consumed with longing for God's law all the time! We are consumed with longing for a lot of things—more money, a different job, to be in better physical shape, a break from the pressures we're under, victory over another person—but when was the last time we were consumed with longing for more time in God's Word?

The law from your mouth is more precious to me than thousands of pieces of silver and gold (Ps. 119:72 NIV).

WOW! Can you imagine? Suppose someone had a winning lottery ticket worth $247 million in their hand, and they offered it to you in exchange for your time in God's Word—would you take it? Some of us might struggle with that, but others would never take the deal. But here's a more difficult (and realistic) test: which do we spend more time thinking about and longing for—money or God's Word? Ouch!

Oh, how I love your law! I meditate on it all day long (Ps. 119:97 NIV).

It's easy for some of us to think that if we spend five to ten minutes a day in "devotions" or "quiet time," we've covered our spiritual bases. But that is not the mindset of a person who delights in the Lord—the Psalmist here describes an all-day focus on His Word. Here's a good comparison. Think back to a time when you received a love note from someone you were **really** interested in. I doubt that you read it only once and then threw it away. You probably read it several times, folded it up, and saved it so you could read it later. And the more serious that interest became, the more often you read the note—several times a day! (Today it's email, an instant message, or a text message that is saved in an electronic file so it can be retrieved later!) I think that's the attitude reflected in this verse.

If I am going to love God's Word enough to meditate on it all day long, it means I am going to set aside a significant chunk of my schedule to study it; and then throughout the day I will reflect back on what I studied and consider how it applies to the situations I'm facing.

> *Spending time with the Lord requires serious time focused in and upon God's Word.*

If you have never studied the Bible in a systematic way and don't have a clue on where to begin, I've included some resources at the end of the chapter that will help.[1]

Some may say, "I just don't have enough time to fit something else in." Hmmm. It seems to me that we make the time for the things that matter most to us.

Spending time with the Lord—cultivating that sense of delight in Him—requires serious time focused in and upon God's Word.

Talking with God

The second aspect of investing time in the Lord is prayer. Again, this is not meeting some five minute obligation each morning so I can earn my spiritual Brownie points for the day or so I can avoid feeling guilty. It's not reciting some formula just before a meal or just before falling asleep. It's not parroting a passage with everyone else in a church service. This is incorporating the reality of communicating with God into every aspect of my whole day—in fact, of my whole life.

Consider these passages:

And pray in the Spirit on all occasions with all kinds of prayers and requests. With this in mind, be alert and always keep on praying for all the saints (Eph. 6:18 NIV).

Paul places this passage at the end of his discussion about putting on the *full armor of God* in order to stand strong in the face of spiritual battle. Some have suggested that he finishes with this emphasis on prayer to show how crucial it is to victory in the struggle. But look at how much Paul stresses prayer in this one verse: *Pray...with all kinds of prayer...and always keep on praying....* We don't have time to do an in-depth analysis of the passage, but it is obvious that the expectation is for us to be deeply committed to prayer as an integral and ongoing part of our lives.

Do not be anxious about anything, but in everything, by prayer and petition, with thanksgiving, present your requests to God (Phil. 4:6 NIV).

Here, Paul demonstrates that every aspect of life is to be taken to the Lord in prayer. He says "in everything." That means "in everything." It's easy for us to see prayer as a last resort—that which we fall back on in crisis when we can't do anything else. But this verse indicates that prayer is to be a first resort—that which we do *before* we do anything else. This would mean praying over every decision we make, every person we hold dear, and every concern we have.

Pray without ceasing (1 Thess. 5:17 ESV).

This may seem like a strange command to us. How can we concentrate on prayer throughout the day when we have to work or go to school? Well, obviously, we shouldn't close our eyes to pray while we are driving to the office, but daily drive times could be an excellent time for prayer—in fact, there are plenty of opportunities throughout the course of a day when we can offer up a prayer of praise or thanksgiving. There are "down" times during the day when we are not required to be concentrating on something else when we might pray for a friend or coworker. There are discretionary moments throughout the day when we are not forced to focus our thoughts on a task—we can take a moment to pray right then. And even when we are engaged in responsibilities, we can ask the Lord to help us in those tasks and perform in a way that pleases Him.

Taking this approach to prayer moves our relationship with the Lord from an occasional brief encounter to an ongoing daily relationship with Him—which is what He designed and desires for us.[2]

Realizing Our Desires

God's promise is sure—when we delight ourselves in Him, He *will* grant us the desires of our heart; but when we start to focus our delight on the Lord, at least two factors kick in that shape and affect the fulfillment of our desires.

First, the more we spend time with the Lord—the more we take delight in Him—the more *our* desires are reshaped to reflect *His* desires. Now, don't think God is playing a trick on us here. It's not a game that He plays where He can get out of His promise. In reality, all of God's desires are good—in fact, they are perfect—so that means all of His desires for us are good. Reshaping our desires so that we are desiring the same things He desires is not some ploy on God's part. It is actually refocusing our desires on the things that are best, the things that are perfect. And as we will see in the next chapter, those things are *very* pleasurable.

But something else happens when we spend time with the Lord. Remember some of the appropriate desires we listed earlier. Some of those are taken care of automatically as we spend more time with the Lord. In Galatians 5:22-23, Paul lists the results of walking with Him: *But the fruit of the Spirit is love, joy, peace, patience, kindness, goodness, faithfulness, gentleness, self-control* (NASB).

If I could package and sell these on the open market, I would be a billionaire —everyone wants at least some of these. But the passage indicates that these are the fruit—the *results*—of walking with God. In the surrounding verses, Paul links these with *walking* by the Spirit (5:16), being *led* by the Spirit (5:18), and *living* by the Spirit (5:25). These verses picture a vital, ongoing, and submissive relationship with God. As we follow Him, He produces these in us!

In other words, as we walk with God—as we delight in Him to that point of redirecting our lives to follow Him—He gives us these desires of our hearts.

> *As we walk with God—as we delight in Him to the point of redirecting our lives to follow Him —He gives us these desires of our heart.*

I understand that this may not be easy; by nature we want to walk our own way. We may look over our shoulders from time to time to see if God is following us, but we like to determine the paths we take. However, what we've seen from these verses is just the opposite.

FINAL THOUGHTS

Even though this may not be easy, it is simple; if we focus our delight on Him and His will for us, the deepest desires of our heart will become reality.

Are you ready to do that? Are you ready to reorder your life so that the sum of your delight is found in Him? Are you ready to invest the time into reading His Word and talking to Him in prayer? Are you ready to cultivate that precious relationship with Him that He makes available to us?

If so, stand back and prepare to experience the desires of your heart in ways you never dreamed possible.

---

1. I recommend *How to Read the Bible for All It's Worth* by Gordon Fee and Douglas Stuart, published by Zondervan, 2003; and *A Basic Guide to Interpreting the Bible: Playing by the Rules* by Robert H. Stein, published by Baker Academic, 1997.

2. An excellent resource for helping you get started on a healthy prayer life is *How to Pray When You Don't Know What to Say* by Elmer L. Towns, published by Regal Books.

NOTES

Chapter Two

Full Joy and Pleasures Forever

OUR NEXT PROMISED BLESSING IS FOUND IN PSALM 16:11…and it is indeed amazing. Here it is:

You make known to me the path of life; in your presence there is fullness of joy; at your right hand are pleasures forevermore (ESV).

Who wouldn't want "fullness of joy" and "pleasures forevermore?" Yet, these blessings are clearly promised and available—to those who meet the conditions.

Think for a moment about complete and full joy—what comes to mind? Celebration? Rejoicing? A party? On the other hand, some might equate it with the absence of several things: fear, anxiety, danger, troubles—and in some cases, even certain people.

What about pleasures forever? When I have taught this section, I have asked what is most often associated with pleasure. Here are some of the answers:

- friends
- vacation
- food
- family
- ice cream
- loving relationships

Of course, you have your own personal list.

To fully appreciate what David was getting at, let's look a little closer at the phrases. When he wrote this song, the word David used for "joy" meant "gladness," "mirth," and "rejoicing." Today we would associate these with hilarity, laughter, and glee. It is used in other verses to express the atmosphere surrounding celebrations, feasts, and festivals. It's the mood you find at major parties and celebrations.

The word he used for "fullness" meant "abundance" and "satisfaction." It was commonly used to express the feeling after eating a large meal—of being "full." Together, this phrase gives the image of having so much joy and rejoicing that we are "full."

Can you imagine dining at the table of joy and consuming so much that you are full and need to push away from the table?

Or imagine that you are a drinking glass and joy was poured into you, filling you up to the very brim! That's the idea behind "fullness of joy."

The word David used for "pleasures" was also used to describe something as "pleasant," "delightful," "sweet," or "lovely." It was used to describe the taste of good food, the nature of a close friendship, and the physical appearance of a lover. Have you ever been around a teenager who *really* liked something and excitedly declared that it was "sweet?" I think that's the idea here. And what makes it even better is that David says these pleasures are nonstop! They are forever!

What a combination—to be filled up to capacity with joy and to be experiencing intense pleasures now and forever.

Now, that is appealing, isn't it? But to experience such things seems like the stuff dreams are made of; we might be tempted to think that these could be available to *some* people, but certainly not to me! Have you ever felt that way?

Like I said, these are blessings that God offers to His children. So what does it take for us to reach the point that we are experiencing such things? What are the essential prerequisites?

If you look to television for the answers, you'll find a variety of options. Commercials declare that these are found in driving the right car, drinking the right brand or kind of beverage, wearing the right make up or jewelry or clothes, eating at the right restaurant, using the right diet plan, exercising at the right club, using the right cell phone service, or securing the right career. TV sitcoms and dramas suggest that these come from being in the "perfect" romantic relationship, pulling off the ideal sexual encounter (even if it is for just one night), deceiving the boss (or spouse), solving an overwhelming problem, or getting revenge.

Game shows and reality programs suggest these come by winning, and sometimes not only by beating but by utterly humiliating the competition. On talk shows we hear repeated over and over that we experience these by taking charge of our lives and pursuing our own dreams; that we should set our sights on these and fully devote ourselves to pursuing joy and pleasure.

But stop and think; you probably know people who are pursuing these. Are they really experiencing the kind of joy and pleasure David is talking about in this passage? If these really held the answer, why aren't more people overwhelmed by joy and pleasure?

The prerequisites to, and essentials for, joy and pleasure are found in the rest of this passage from Psalms. We don't have time to do an in-depth study of the whole chapter, but in these verses we find several basic requirements that must be met before we can experience the richness of these blessings. In these verses, we find that this kind of joy and pleasure can never be found by pursuit, they can only be found as a result— they are the result of pursuing and experiencing the prerequisites.

ONE—AND ONLY ONE—GOD

In the first few verses of this chapter we find not

only an essential prerequisite, but the foundation for all real joy and pleasure. It is the reality and practice of serving only one God. Embracing this truth may seem like a "no brainer" to us, but when we examine the implications and how they apply to us, we will see that, while the truth of it may be simple, following David's example is not so easy.

David declares in verse 2: *I say to the* LORD, *"You are my Lord; I have no good apart from you"* (ESV).

The title "Lord" is used twice in this verse, but look at the difference between them. The first time, the title is spelled out in all uppercase letters, and in the second only the "L" is uppercase.

Have you ever noticed that difference before? You will find it throughout the Old Testament; it is a common way English translators distinguish between the different names of God. Whenever you find "LORD," it is being used for *Yahweh*, the name by which God identified Himself to Moses at the burning bush. On the other hand, whenever you find "Lord," it's usually translating another Hebrew name for God: *Adonai.*

In this passage, David is proclaiming to the God of Abraham, Isaac, Jacob, and Moses that He is his one, true God. In verse 4 he emphasizes his commitment to not "run after another god."

This seems so obvious to us—of course God would be his one and only God! But in David's day, such a statement set him apart from all of the other kings, cultures, and religious influences of the day. Israel was the only monotheistic nation in the known world at the time—they were an oddity to all of the other nations who had hundreds, and sometimes thousands, of gods from which to choose.

The pagan nations expected these gods to care for every conceivable aspect and need of life: health, the economy, national security, crops, procreation, national direction, provisions, you name it. If there was a need, the people had come up with various gods to meet that need. And typically, worshipping those false gods led to sexual perversion, materialism, and pride. Even more, they led to the devaluation and destruction of human life.

God delivered Israel from slavery in Egypt, a nation that worshipped a host of gods. He established a covenant with Israel at Mount Sinai in which they were expected (rightly so) to reject all other options and follow only one God Who would not only provide for all of their needs, but would be their ultimate authority. But He was about to lead them into a new land where all the people worshipped many gods, so he warned them to avoid the lure of looking away from God and falling into idolatry. The danger was that if they were not careful, the Israelites would start to view the LORD as only one god among many.

Yet, after they entered and conquered Canaan, they began to be enticed by these other gods. From studying the Scriptures, I summarize idolatry as redirecting one's faith, focus, and affection away from God. The Israelites began to direct their faith, focus, and affections from the one, true God to other false gods. In the years leading up to the reign of David, the Israelites had cycled back and forth between their devotion to God and their descent into idolatry.

But David was a man after God's own heart. There was no doubt in his own mind—he was absolutely devoted to keeping his eyes and heart set upon the LORD. The joy and pleasure he speaks of at the end of this psalm could never have become reality apart from this prerequisite.

So, what about today? Surely there aren't other gods that would compete for our faith, focus, and affection—are there?

Well, in today's America it is not difficult to find a number of growing religions that worship a god (or gods) that are clearly in competition with the Lord. If you were to ask a Muslim cleric (an Imam), you would discover that the Allah of Islam is not the same person as the God of the Bible. My Baha'i neighbor's concept of god is entirely different from what the Bible teaches. And Hindus and some Buddhists would inform you that there is not only one God, but many. Each of these faiths is growing in the United States and their adherents worship gods that stand in stark contrast to the God revealed in the Bible.

Faith

But these are not the only threats to our loyalty to God—there are many things in our society and culture that can threaten to divert our faith, our trust and confidence, away from God. Whereas the Canaanites trusted false gods for their health, we can easily place misdirected trust in science or the medical industry.

For our economy, we can be tempted to trust the Fed and our investments. For national security, of course we look to our government and military forces. For our income, we're tempted to place our full trust in our employers. For national direction, we are inclined to trust our elected officials.

In His position and role as God, He is the only one in Whom we should place our full faith—not just for salvation, but for all aspects of life.

And for the major decisions of life, we trust...ourselves—our own abilities to decide by ourselves what's best for us.

But we all know full well that none of these are absolutely reliable—they all can fail, and, in fact, they all *have* failed. None are worthy of our absolute faith.

Don't get me wrong—it is appropriate to seek the advice of medical doctors for medical problems; to strive to make wise investments; to seek sound, stable, and gainful employment; to elect moral, capable, and competent leaders for government positions.

What is inappropriate is when we place our ultimate and final confidence in these areas or individuals rather than God, forgetting to ask Him first for guidance in each area and forgetting that He holds all of these in His hand and that He alone is worthy of our absolute trust. In His position and role as God, He is the only one in Whom we should place our full faith—not just for salvation, but for all aspects of life.

Focus

Our focus also can easily shift from God as our ultimate and final authority to ourselves. We are a nation of rugged individuals who rely on no one and nothing else besides ourselves. We are expected and encouraged to be the masters of our own destiny and to shun outside assistance. The world preaches that we should be able to make it on our own. By nature, we resist authority and are inclined toward independence, autonomy, and self rule.

We embrace the notion that it is better to ask forgiveness than permission.

Of course, we realize that heaven and hell are outside the realm of our control, so we are naturally more inclined to look to God for deliverance from hell. But until the time comes for us to cross over to the afterlife, we are content to call all of the shots here in this life. But here's the problem: that mindset defies the reality of Who God is and of His absolute right to have full authority over every aspect of our lives.

Affection

Furthermore, our affection can be drawn away from the Lord by any number of competitors: comfort, material possessions, recognition, accomplishments, hobbies, love interests—you know what they are, you fill in the blanks. There is no shortage of things that threaten to shift our affection away from the Lord.

Yet, to have one, and only one God, as David declares in this verse, means that He is the primary object of our affection, and that all other affections and desires fall in line behind Him. If we are to be consumed or obsessed, it should be with Him rather than our own desires.

To have only one God—an irrefutable prerequisite to full joy and eternal pleasures—means turning away from all other gods, and everything that would compete with God, and giving our hearts fully to Him.

Every other essential in this passage is built upon this foundational requirement.

Safe Refuge

In verse 1, David pleads with God and declares: *Preserve me, O God, for in you I take refuge* (ESV).

David could have sought refuge in his military, his position as king, or his own devices, but he knew where his real protection was found.

When the pressures and problems of this world attack us, sometimes we are inclined to seek refuge from man-made sources: our investment accounts, friendships, family, government, or (most often) our own ingenuity and ability.

The problem is, we are not big enough to fight the enemy, regardless of how much we might try to convince ourselves otherwise—and that is humbling.

Joy and pleasure are directly linked to recognizing and turning to Him first as our refuge.

Delight in the Saints

The next essential may seem odd to us. In verse 3, David exclaims: *As for the saints in the land, they are the excellent ones, in whom is all my delight* (ESV).

David wasn't speaking about heroes of the faith that had gone before him; he was talking about those around him who were faithful in following the Lord. He held them in high esteem and viewed them as a great source of delight.

So often we seek joy and pleasure in private things and individual pursuits. But here, as strange as it may seem, David demonstrates that the richest joys and pleasures are linked to community; more specifically, to active interaction and participation with a community of faith in which the members are sincerely striving to be faithful to one, and only one, God.

I know some are reading this and saying that it just doesn't make sense. Many of us know what it is like to be scorned by hypocrites in a church. Honestly, not every church measures up to the standard from this passage. There are plenty of churches that are filled with a majority of people who are pursuing their own agendas and have no interest in directing their faith, focus, and affection to the Lord. Church, for them, is a place where religious people gather to enjoy religious music, hear religious messages from a religious preacher, and if absolutely necessary, participate in a few token religious activities.

There are few places on earth that are closer to

hell than these. In fact, some of the worst strip joints and red light districts in the country may be closer to heaven!

That's not what David is talking about. Please trust me when I tell you that there is no describing the pure delight that comes from being with others who sincerely love God and love each other, and who are committed to striving to grow together in Him.

And there are churches where the pastor and majority of the members share this goal—you just have to look a little harder to find them.

Seek His Counsel

In verse 7, David says: *I bless the LORD who gives me counsel; in the night also my heart instructs me* (ESV).

Where do we get our counsel and advice? About:

+ employment
+ finances and investments
+ romance and marriage
+ friendships
+ child raising
+ direction in life

When I've asked this in class, there have been two

common responses: Oprah and Dr. Phil. But as popular as they may be, neither is offering the resources to give full joy and eternal pleasures.

David sets the right example by seeking counsel from God—which only makes sense. Think about it—God possesses all the wisdom and knowledge in the universe. He made us! He knows what makes us tick. He knows what the future holds, He knows what we need, He cares about us, and He truly wants what is best for us. But so often we are like little children who insist to their mom that *they* know what is best for themselves and don't need their mother's help.

Experiencing true joy and pleasure requires that we look first to God for direction. And where do we find His direction? Psalm 119:105 says: *Your word is a lamp to my feet and a light to my path* (ESV). Have you ever been deep down in a cave or out in the forest late at night when the moon is not shining? If you have ever been in real darkness, you appreciate the value of a flashlight. The world around us is a dark place, and God offers His Word

> *The world around us is a dark place, and God offers His Word as a light.*

as a light. This is the starting point in finding God's counsel.

In addition to Bible study, the Scriptures also say we should ask God for wisdom and that He readily gives it to those who trust Him (Jas. 1:5,6). Here we see again how Bible study and prayer are so essential to experiencing God's richest blessings. These are the primary resources God gives for direction, and the more we look to Him for counsel, the more time we will spend in each.

LIVING IN HIS PRESENCE

In verses 8 and 16, we find the final essential for joy and pleasure. Here David says: *I have set the LORD always before me; because he is at my right hand, I shall not be shaken.* (16:8 ESV)

You make known to me the path of life; in your presence there is fullness of joy; at your right hand are pleasures forevermore. (16:11 ESV)

In both of these verses, we find a common emphasis: dwelling in the presence of God. In verse 8, David said that he was "always" in his presence. David lived life in the presence of God. For him, God was not an occasional experience or someone he talked to on rare occasion. Even more importantly, God was not someone to Whom David ran as a last resort when he was in desperate need. Other passages tell us that David loved God deeply and treasured the time he could spend with Him.

What a stark contrast to how we often view our relationship with God. It is so easy to see Him as someone we go to when we have an emergency—like a heavenly fireman or EMT. Or, we look at Him as the One Who grants our wishes and desires—like a divine Santa Claus or fairy godmother.

On the other hand, some of us may be afraid to go to Him. We may see Him as cruel and harsh, waiting for us to come into His presence so He can crush us or make us miserable.

The incredible truth about God is that He truly deserves to be our one and only God—the Almighty God of the universe Who alone is worthy of all of our faith, focus, and affection. But at the same time, He also is approachable—indeed, according to this passage, it is in His very presence that we find fullness of joy and pleasures forever.

Final Thoughts

God wants His children to experience fullness of joy and eternal pleasures, but these are not found in ways the world tells us.

God is so different than what we typically envision. He stands ready to bless us in some pretty amazing ways. Again, it may not be what we expected, or the way we expected it, but to those who come to Him this way, the joy and pleasure is absolutely indescribable!

Are you there yet? Are you experiencing these blessings first hand? If not, now you know—it's time to go for it. Run to Him as your one and only God. Pour all of your faith, focus, and affection on Him. Trust Him as your safe refuge. Celebrate with the saints who are doing the same. Go to Him first for your counsel. Live all of your life in His presence.

Then...watch out!

NOTES

Chapter Three

Absolute Victory Over Satan

THE NEXT BLESSING, ONE THAT IS especially important today, is found in the Gospel According to Matthew:

And I tell you, you are Peter, and on this rock I will build my church, and the gates of hell shall not prevail against it (16:18 ESV).

Here, Jesus promises that His followers have the opportunity to partake in absolute and ultimate victory over Satan and all his forces.

The Darkness That Surrounds Us

There is no shortage of evidence that Satan is at work around us. Years ago, Hal Lindsey wrote the book *Satan is Alive and Well on Planet Earth*. If that title were accurate then, how much more so is it today? All we have to do is look around to see his handiwork.

Pervading Immorality

It's no secret that immorality is being normalized around us. Fifty years ago the vast majority of people in our country would have recognized homosexuality as wrong. Today, it is increasingly portrayed by the media and political figures as normative and as an acceptable alternative lifestyle. Over that same time period, sexual norms have shifted downward so that unwed teen pregnancy is not only acceptable in society, it is even desirable to many young girls. Pornography has become a multi-billion dollar industry. Human trafficking with its related sexual slavery has become a lucrative business in our land.

Fascination with the Occult

Media interest in the occult seems to be at an

all-time high. When in our history has there been such a roster of television programs focusing primarily and specifically on themes of the occult? For the last few years, smaller markets have released programs such as *Buffy the Vampire Killer* and *Supernatural*, but today on the primary networks you find titles such as *Medium* and *Ghost Whisperer*. On the big screen and on video, there are countless releases dealing even more specifically with demons and their master. The dark side is really big business.

Collapse of Family Structure

Divorce proceedings are virtually as common as marriage ceremonies in today's society. Fifty years ago the vast majority of children were raised in families with two parents, both of whom were biologically related to the children. Today, that environment is no longer the norm—single-parent homes and step-families compete for that designation. And a domestic option that was unimaginable fifty years ago—families with two mommies or two daddies—has forced its way into the social and legal arena, demanding to be recognized and accepted as normal.

Domestic Terrorism

Prior to 9/11, the notion of a broad-based threat of terrorism in our homeland was the stuff of obscure, late-night radio talk shows. Today, we understand that there are people in this world who are anxious to destroy us just because we are Americans. In fact, if it were not for massive and monumental efforts to prevent it, those attacks on our land in September, 2001, would have only been the beginning. In these attacks we can see the face of evil up close—when we look carefully at such deeds, we stare into the very eyes of malevolence. And while we can hardly bear to look at something so vile and detestable, we know that if we look away it will pounce upon us and devour our nation.

Evidence of the enemy's presence and activity is undeniable for anyone willing to face reality.

Evidence of the enemy's presence and activity is undeniable for anyone willing to face reality.

How are we to survive in the face of such an onslaught from the enemy? The threat is so ominous and pervasive—if it weren't for this promise in Matthew, we might be tempted to give up hope.

But in this promise from Jesus, we find assurance that we can experience ultimate and total victory.

Jesus said that "the gates of hell will not prevail" against His church. We don't refer to a city's gates in today's culture, but in Jesus' day a city's strength was directed toward its gates—that was where all of the power and fortification were found. When Jesus used the phrase, it represented all the darkest and most terrible powers of hell—but His promise is that all of these powers will ultimately fail in their quest to defeat and destroy God's people. In this promise we find the absolute confidence that no matter how bleak the situations around us may seem, no matter how dark the circumstances, Satan will not win—he is destined for total defeat.

THE PLACE OF VICTORY

But how can we share in that victory? What must we do to experience that blessing of seeing the enemy's efforts ultimately fail? Some would say that we are to go about "binding" Satan and his demons, shouting emotional proclamations and sometimes screaming passionate condemnations. The problem with that view is it isn't supported by Scripture.[1] In fact, the Bible warns against getting carried away with such things (Jude 8, 9).

Others might say that we experience victory by staying "prayed up" and living a chaste life—and while both are extremely important, they are not the primary key to the massive victory Jesus talks about.

In this passage, Jesus directly links this monumental victory to one element—His church. The confident assurance is that Jesus' plans for His church will not be thwarted or threatened in any way by even the strongest forces of spiritual darkness. All that He wants to accomplish in and through His church will ultimately succeed, despite the arsenal at the enemy's disposal.

That means ultimate victory is not tied to individual efforts, but to the corporate body—the church.

This flies in the face of our Western mindset—we pride ourselves in our strength and rugged individualism, and that flawed perspective makes its way into our churches far too easily. There are some among us who would promote a "special-ops forces" mentality, as if we could go through some sort of spiritual boot camp to receive specialized training for hand-to-hand combat with the spiritual enemy. It is dramatic and sensational to fancy ourselves as Christian versions of Rambo, faces painted with some sort of spiritual camouflage, storming the gates of hell and single-handedly wreaking havoc on the forces of evil.

Such thinking is not only flawed, it is dangerous. It falls right into the hands of the enemy and leads to certain destruction—because it is arrogant. It connects the victory to individual efforts and bravado, not the Lord's power and plan. And the enemy delights in our arrogance because *God is opposed to the proud, but gives grace to the humble.*

Satan eats such self-styled "warriors" every day for lunch.

Ultimate victory over the enemy is not experienced individually, but corporately. For us to experience the victory Jesus speaks of in this passage, we must be plugged into His church. Only there can we experience such triumph.

Now don't rush down to that building on the corner with the steeple on top and think that you are safe there from spiritual attacks. That may be where His church gathers, but that is not what Jesus is talking about in this passage.

So just what is Jesus talking about in this passage? What must we do to be a part of this church and participate in the glorious victory He promises?

COMING TO THE KING AND HIS CHURCH

This portion of Scripture begins with Jesus asking His disciples some important and defining questions. He had been wildly popular at the beginning of His ministry with thousands following Him, but over the course of His ministry He failed to live up to some popular expectations. John the Baptist had pointed to Him as the promised Messiah, and consequently many were expecting Jesus to lead a revolution against Rome. But when King Herod imprisoned and executed John, many began to question whether or not Jesus was truly the Promised One.

On top of that, some of His teaching was offensive even to some who had followed Him closely, and many deserted Him.[2] His popularity started to wane and the numbers of His followers started to dwindle. It would have been easy for the Twelve to be alarmed at the shift in momentum and to start second guessing their decision to leave everything and follow Him.

In this context, Jesus asks them: *Who do people say that the Son of Man is?* (Matt. 16:13 ESV).

In the next two verses we find the following exchange: *And they said, "Some say John the Baptist, others say Elijah, and others Jeremiah or one of the prophets." He said to them, "But who do you say that I am?" Simon Peter replied, "You are the Christ, the Son of the living God"* (Matt. 16:14-17 ESV).

In Peter's response on behalf of the other disciples, we find the heart of the whole issue. It is in his answer that we find our answer to being a part of His church and experiencing ultimate victory. Peter proclaimed that Jesus was the *Christ, the Son of the Living God.*

That phrase may mean very little to us today, but in the first century it was about as bold and insightful a statement as anyone could make. For Peter and the disciples to unhesitatingly identify Jesus this way was for them to declare their absolute allegiance and commitment to Jesus as King and Lord.

Let me explain.

Today, we treat the name *Christ* as if it were the second half of Jesus' name—almost as if it were His last name. But for first-century Jews, the terms *Christ,*

Messiah, and *king* were synonymous. From the Hebrew prophecies, they knew the Messiah—the Christ (which meant *anointed one*)—was to come and reign as king over not only Israel, but the whole earth. Peter was recognizing Jesus as the promised King Who would reign over them.

Again, today in the United States, we don't appreciate all that was represented by the title *king*. As I have observed in another work, "For the most part we dismiss kings and kingdoms as the stuff of ancient history and children's fairy tales."[3] Not so for those who lived in the first century. Their view of kings and kingdoms shaped their very existence.[4]

Majesty and Deity

In ancient cultures everyone understood that there was a divine link between the king and deity. In some cases, the people viewed the king as the divinely appointed ruler. In others, he was viewed as an extension of particular gods or even as a priest. Sometimes, the king was viewed as being a god himself.

In Jesus' day, under the culture and beliefs of Rome, Caesar was worshipped as one of many gods.

Before the Romans ruled over Israel, the Greek ruler Antiochus Epiphanies, which means "Antiochus the God is Manifest," entered Jerusalem and sacrificed a pig on the temple altar. In doing this, he was not only elevating the worship of Zeus over the worship of *Yahweh*, he was also flexing his own divine muscle.

But think back to before the Greeks ruled—do you remember why Daniel was thrown in the lion's den? It was because he refused to pray to King Darius. And why were Shadrach, Meshach, and Abednego thrown into the fiery furnace? Because they refused to bow down in worship before the image of Nebuchadnezzar. These cultures all viewed the kings as deities.

But the Jews knew that all of these kings were fake deities and that when the promised Messiah arrived, He would be the ultimate King—because He was truly from God and was truly God.

When Peter made this declaration, he was affirming the disciples' conviction that Jesus as Messiah/King was indeed Divine.

Absolute Authority

Next, because of this divine connection, the king

was the absolute, ultimate, and final authority—typically he not only determined the law, he *was* the law. Whatever the king desired and decreed became reality. From a personal and practical standpoint, this had a direct bearing on all the inhabitants of the corresponding kingdom. If the king wanted more money, the people were taxed more heavily. If he wanted additional labor, he could force his subjects to work for little or nothing. If he wanted a man's life, that man was doomed—there was no higher court to which he could appeal. The king held the people in his hand and could do with them as he chose.

The Jewish people had vivid images of such kings over the centuries and even in the time of Jesus.

The Pharaoh of Exodus 1 could enslave an entire segment of people living in the land and call for the death of every male Jewish baby. Similarly, centuries later, Herod "the Great" could order the slaughter of every male child in Bethlehem and the surrounding area under the age of two. About thirty years later, his son, Herod Antipas, arrested John the Baptist because he didn't like his preaching and eventually had him beheaded at the request of two wicked women. Such actions were entirely consistent with the absolute authority inherent in the position—kings had the right to do such things. No one could take their appeal to another level—the king *was* the supreme court.

Ultimate Ownership

Finally, because of his divine authority it was common for the king to assume ultimate ownership of everything in his kingdom—land, animals, and even the people.

Of course, a wise king might allow certain merchants to trade independently, and he might grant provisional ownership of land to those he valued or whom he wanted to reward, but everyone knew the king had ultimate ownership and could take possession of anything, at any time. Such a perspective is evident in Jezebel's criticism of King Ahab for not taking possession of Naboth's property (1 Kings 21:7).

And, of course, if there was resistance to any of these, the king commanded an army that would execute his wishes.

Peter and the disciples believed they had found the ultimate and true combination of these three components—they believed they were fully prepared to recognize and submit to Jesus' deity, authority, and ownership.

Peter was not merely reciting the obvious; on behalf of the other eleven disciples he was acknowledging and affirming the Lord's right to have absolute rule over every aspect of their lives and declaring their full submission to that right. He did not merely recognize Jesus' *title* as King, he fully acknowledged His *role* as King.

You see, to identify and declare that a person is king is to automatically declare full allegiance and submission to that person. For Peter to identify and declare Jesus as King was to indicate that he recognized and worshipped Him as God, that he fully submitted to His authority, and that he fully yielded to His ownership.

In response, Jesus not only affirmed Peter's statement and commended Him for it; He went on to make a statement that should radically transform our understanding of the church. In verses 17-18, He said:

"Blessed are you, Simon Barjona, because flesh and blood did not reveal this to you, but My Father who is in

heaven. I also say to you that you are Peter, and upon this rock I will build My church; and the gates of Hades will not overpower it" (NASB).

Jesus' response to Peter is one of the most debated passages in the history of the church, but I fear in all of the debate we have overlooked an essential point of the Lord's response. For centuries, Christians have debated the identity of the "rock" upon which Jesus would build the church. The Catholic Church has held that the rock is Peter. Some assert that Jesus is identifying Himself as the rock. Others say that because Peter was speaking on behalf of the disciples, Jesus identified the group collectively as the rock. Still others suggest that Peter's statement alone is the rock.

However, the identification of the rock is not nearly as important for us as the reality associated with it. No matter which of these options (or others) eventually proves to be the rock, the reality is that the foundation upon which Jesus builds His church is directly and inseparably linked to the recognition of and submission to Jesus as the absolute King!

New Testament scholar Craig Blomberg observed about this passage: "...Christ's 'church' will comprise the community of people who submit to God's kingly rule…."[5]

Jesus' intention is obvious and unavoidable: His followers were to fully recognize and submit to Him as King, and it was *those* followers who would comprise the church.

In Peter's statement we find the identification of Jesus as King with the corresponding absolute surrender to His Kingship. In Jesus' statement we find the essential link between this recognition, and corresponding surrender, to the nature of the church as Jesus planned it. The implications are both indisputable and astounding: A true church is made up of those who are willing to recognize and submit to Jesus as King!

A true church is made up of those who are willing to recognize and submit to Jesus as King.

In fact, an assembly that is made up mostly of religious people who are not recognizing and submitting to the King may be a religious gathering, but it is not a church according to Jesus' definition, regardless of what it calls itself.

And it is *this* church—the body of those who are recognizing and submitting to the King—that experiences the spiritual victory over the enemy promised by the Lord, not the religious gathering.

IMPLICATIONS AND APPLICATIONS

The first implication relates to each one of us in our relationship with the Lord. It is very easy to view Jesus as merely the One Who rescues me—He rescued me from hell when He died on the cross, and He rescues me whenever I have a crisis.

But Jesus did not come to earth merely as some heavenly lifeguard who jumps into the water to save us whenever we get in over our heads. The reality is that He is the Sovereign King of the universe, and we ought to view and revere Him as such.

That means at least three things: first, because He combines ultimate majesty and deity, we should treat Him with the highest respect, reverence, and honor. We don't treat Him as our "buddy," and we don't address Him as a casual friend. He's the KING! Yes, He is tender and loving in His dealings with us, and He calls those who follow Him His friends, but that does not mean we are to mistake this as an invitation to treat Him as an equal. He is not—as King, He is worthy of all our honor, exaltation, adoration, and highest respect. We dare not try to reduce Him to our level—He's the King.

Second, because He is the King, He is to have absolute authority over every aspect of our lives. That means that we don't decide, all on our own, what career we will pursue and then ask Him to bless our decision; we go to the King and ask what He would have us do. We don't tell Him what home we are going to buy and ask Him to bless the purchase; we ask Him what He would like and for guidance in finding the right home. When looking for a spouse, we don't hand Him our profile of a perfect spouse and ask Him to provide that person; we ask Him to lead us to the one He wants for us.

And when He commands us through His Word to do something, the proper response is: "Yes, Your Majesty."

Can you imagine a king commanding a subject to do something for him and the subject responding: "Oh, I wish I could—I really do—but I just don't have enough time. You understand, don't you?"

I don't think so.

But isn't that how we respond to Jesus sometimes? We know that He expects us to love those who may not be so easy to love, but we complain to Him about how hard it is and expect Him to excuse us because of the "special circumstances" surrounding our situation. We know that He expects us to tell the truth, but we complain to Him about the uncomfortable consequences that would follow, and then we expect Him to let us off the hook. We know that He doesn't want us to lose our temper, but we remind Him that this is "just the way I am," and that He made us,

In every command regarding every aspect of life, the correct response is: "Yes, Your Majesty."

so He should understand. It is so easy for us to expect the King to cater to our desires, forgetting that it is supposed to be just the opposite.

In every command regarding every aspect of life, the correct response is: "Yes, Your Majesty."

Finally, because He is King, He has full ownership over every aspect of our lives. This is really hard, I know, but this is the way it is supposed to be. It's not my checkbook, it's His, and He has every right to do with that money what He desires. It's not my house, it is His, and He deserves for me to use it for His glory. They are not my children, they are His, and He has every right to expect me to raise them the way that pleases Him the most. And it's not my life, it's His, and He is free to do whatever he pleases with it.

Now remember, He is good, He is loving, He is compassionate and gracious, He is tender and forgiving—so we can trust Him completely as we surrender everything over to Him, but we still are expected to surrender everything over to Him...because He is the King.

Embracing that reality is essential if we really want to be in a position to see His absolute victory over Satan.

The second implication relates to our participation in His church—again, the victory in this passage is not associated with fighting the enemy individually, but rather it is directly tied to His church. To realize this aspect of the promise, we are required to become a part of His church.

That doesn't happen by staying home and watching preachers on television each week. It means finding a church with people who share these convictions—who are more committed to obeying and serving the King than they are to building their own kingdom—and joining them. This isn't just attending services, it means becoming an active part of that community of faith. And as I said in the last chapter, it may be difficult to find this kind of church, but if you ask the King to lead you to such a church, He will—He knows right where they are!

FINAL THOUGHTS

So, there it is. We have the option of experiencing and participating in the greatest victory over Satan since the cross—and that victory is sure! But we won't taste it fully unless we are fully prepared to recognize and submit to the Kingship of Jesus and then plug into His church. But what a trade-off! Only a fool would turn down that benefit because he thought it wasn't worth the price! Remember, the alternative is to taste certain misery and defeat ourselves!

What a wonderful Savior—what a glorious King! We can sing along with Moses: *Who among the gods is* like you, O LORD? Who is like you—majestic in holiness, awesome in glory, working wonders? (Ex. 15:11 NIV). We can declare along with John: *Greater is He that is in you, than he that is in the world* (1 John 4:4 KJV). And we can celebrate along with Paul: *He who is the blessed and only Sovereign, the King of kings and Lord of lords, who alone possesses immortality and dwells in unapproachable light, Whom no man has seen or can see. To Him be honor and eternal dominion! Amen* (1 Tim. 6:15-16 NASB).

And Amen!

---

1. For an excellent discussion of "loosing and binding" see Blomberg's discussion in *The New American Commentary*, "Matthew," (Nashville: Broadman Press, 1993), 254,255.

2. John 6.

3. *The Forgotten Command—Make Disciples; Rediscovering and Embracing the Heart of the Great Commission* by John Revell, scheduled for release in 2009.

4. The following comes from *The Forgotten Command*.

5. Blomberg, 253.

NOTES

Chapter Four

Expanded Family, Houses, and Land

THE FINAL BLESSING WE'LL EXPLORE sounds pretty amazing. In this passage from Mark, the Lord promises that if we meet certain conditions we will receive some pretty astounding blessings:

Jesus said, "Truly, I say to you, there is no one who has left house or brothers or sisters or mother or father or children or lands, for my sake and for the gospel, who will not receive a hundredfold now in this time, houses and brothers and sisters and mothers and children and lands, with persecutions, and in the age to come eternal life (10:29-30 ESV).

Did you catch that? Jesus promised expanded families, houses, and land a hundredfold!!! Why haven't we heard more about this?! That's astounding! Why aren't more preachers talking about this from the pulpit?!

It's probably because this emphasis is sandwiched between two unpleasant realities that leave us feeling a little uncomfortable—and make many preachers feel even more uncomfortable. On one side of the promise is the reality of the sacrifice required in following Him; on the other is the promise of persecution.

Ouch—that doesn't sound so good, does it?

I admit, this sounds really strange. What on earth was Jesus talking about? Is this a real promise? And if so, what about the sacrifice and persecution? Is the blessing worth the cost?

Let's look at the whole passage to find out.

THE RICH YOUNG RULER

Jesus' statements come at the end of an encounter and conversation with a wealthy young man described in other accounts as being a "ruler." Bible scholars suggest that he was probably a high official in the local synagogue. In the Jewish culture, wealth was viewed as a blessing from God that was directly linked to a person's righteousness, and holding a position of religious leadership meant God was especially pleased with him. In everyone's mind, this man was the poster boy for righteousness and blessings. He had it all: possessions, prestige, youth, and God's obvious hand of blessing upon Him.

But apparently he felt that he was missing something, because the passage says that one day he ran up to Jesus, knelt before Him, and asked: "What must I do to inherit eternal life?" (10:17). Jesus responded: *You know the commandments: "Do not murder, Do not commit adultery, Do not steal, Do not bear false witness, Do not defraud, Honor your father and mother"* (10:19 ESV).

The young man answered that he had kept all of those commands from his youth.

Jesus then responded: *You lack one thing: go, sell all that you have and give to the poor, and you will have treasure in heaven; and come, follow me* (10:21 ESV).

These verses, and the verses that follow, show us at least three essentials if we would like to partake of the blessings mentioned at the beginning of the chapter.

Rejecting Empty Religious Ritual

In this conversation, Jesus confirmed what the young man was sensing: going through the motions of keeping a religious set of standards leaves you empty, unfulfilled, and spiritually inadequate. This man had devoted his life to maintaining an external set of religious standards without embracing the heart—the very Person—behind those standards.

I can't really blame him for holding that view—that's how he was raised. The religious leaders of the day emphasized that righteousness was attained by keeping all of the meticulous details of the Jewish laws. This man had grown up learning and keeping the Ten Commandments, and he was taught that this was the essence of righteousness. When Jesus listed these five commands it was an easy test for the man, and Jesus knew how he would respond.

But the young synagogue official knew something was wrong with what he had learned and been living. He would never have approached Jesus if he had been experiencing a strong sense of spiritual fulfillment and assurance. Something was missing, and he was struggling to find out what that was.

You may have grown up in a similar environment; maybe not focusing on the finer points of the Jewish law, but picking up the sense that being a good person—or even a good Christian—was a matter of keeping a list of "dos and don'ts." The phrase I learned as a young person in the South was "I don't drink, I don't smoke, I don't chew, and I don't go out with girls that do!" For many, such a creed would summarize the essence of their religious faith—a very empty, impersonal faith that ignores the Person behind all moral standards.

That mindset is at work in those who base the depth of their spirituality on the level of their church activities—those who are viewed as "most spiritual" are the ones who attend the most church services, put the most in the offering plate, and are serving on the most church committees. And if they teach the middle-school boys' Sunday School class, they are super spiritual!

But a religion that focuses primarily on our level of religious activity is man-centered, not God-centered. It elevates our own performance rather than God's grace—and while that kind of religion may be self-gratifying for awhile, ultimately it will fall short, leaving us to come face to face with our own spiritual inadequacy.

To experience the richest blessings that God offers His children means turning from mere religious ritual and turning to a Person—Jesus Christ.

Fully Surrendering Our Treasures

Jesus' second response to this man cut to the heart of his problem. He lifted up a lantern and shined it into the deepest part of that young man's heart when He told him to sell his possessions, give the proceeds to the poor, and follow Him. But the most telling statement was that if he did he would have treasures in heaven.

The passage goes on to say that this poor rich man was "disheartened" by Jesus' words and left His presence a very sad man.

Of course, Jesus understood all that was at work in this man's life when he approached. That may be why He didn't list the first five commands which begin with "You shall have no other gods before me." He understood that this man's treasure was tied to all of his possessions. That is confirmed by the man's reaction and departure. If the man had had no other gods but the LORD, he would have responded differently—it's clear that his faith, focus, and affection were directed to himself and his own possessions, rather than to the Lord. He was clinging desperately to his possessions, refusing to let go.

When he left, Jesus commented on just how difficult it was for a rich man to enter the Kingdom of heaven—that it would be easier for a camel to go through the eye of a needle than for a rich man to enter the kingdom.

His point was not that a person of material wealth could not be saved, but that it was extremely difficult because the rich tend to treasure their wealth.

Back then wealth symbolized so much—it represented success and God's favor, projecting to everyone the accomplishments of that person. But for someone to truly follow the Lord, it takes viewing Jesus and His Kingdom as true wealth. A person who is devoted to one, and only one, God views Him as the ultimate treasure and would gladly surrender anything and everything over to Him.

> *A person who is devoted to the one, and only one, God views Him as the ultimate treasure.*

This rich young ruler had recognized the emptiness of religious ritual, but he was not willing to take that critical step necessary to move beyond it to true righteousness. He was not willing to recognize Jesus as King, surrendering everything over to Him and placing his focus on heavenly treasures rather than earthly possessions.

Following Him, Regardless of the Cost

Does Jesus command all of His followers to sell all of their possessios? Well, not exactly. (I can hear the collective sigh of relief.)

Jesus commanded this man to sell everything because He knew his heart was wrapped around his wealth. He hasn't commanded all of His followers to sell all their possessions and give the proceeds to the poor; yet, He consistently demonstrated a deep concern for those in need and expected His followers to do the same, and remember from last chapter that He is the King—the King has absolute ownership of everything—so He would certainly have the right to give that command.

But He *has* given the broad command that anyone

who would follow Him must be willing to sacrifice anything and everything for Him. In Matthew 16, following the discussion with Peter concerning His identity, Jesus said:

If anyone wishes to come after Me, he must deny himself, and take up his cross and follow Me. For whoever wishes to save his life will lose it; but whoever loses his life for My sake will find it. For what will it profit a man if he gains the whole world and forfeits his soul? Or what will a man give in exchange for his soul? (24-26 NASB).

Here Jesus indicates that those who wish to be identified with Him must do three things: First, they must deny "self." That does not mean denying myself *something*, such as a Snickers bar or my favorite bowl of ice cream, it means denying *self*. For me to deny self means I must recognize that He is in charge and that I am not. It is all about Him, not me. It means seeing Him as the center of my universe, not me. It means He is the King—I am not.

Second, followers must take up their crosses. Today, to refer to something as the "cross that I must bear" usually means that it is a particular burden, such as: "My mother-in-law is the cross I have to bear." (Certainly, I am not referring to my own mother-in-law—she is a delightful woman whom I love dearly—but not everyone is as blessed as I am. I just wanted to clear that up.)

In the first century, everyone recognized the cross as a symbol of execution—it was associated with death. Those who heard Jesus' comments knew that He expected His followers to be willing and prepared to die for Him. Of course, those who view Jesus as King would not have a problem with that, because that is the proper mindset for a person to have toward his or her king.

Third, Jesus expected His disciples to follow Him—wherever He would lead. That might not seem like a problem—until He leads us somewhere we don't want to go!

Typically, we want Jesus to follow us around to rescue us when we get into trouble and to bless us when we ask for it. But that's not what Jesus had in mind. Jesus' expectation is that His disciples would follow Him, even when He leads to places that are undesirable, or frightening, or dangerous. And what makes it even more difficult is that He doesn't tell us upfront where we are going! He just tells us to follow Him. Of course, that takes trust; you don't willingly follow someone if you don't know where you are going or what you will encounter—unless you really trust that person.

So, while Jesus may not have given a specific command to all of His followers to sell all of their possessions and give all the proceeds to the poor, He made it very clear that following Him meant recognizing His absolute authority over our lives and being willing to do whatever He commanded, no matter how great the sacrifice, even if it meant dying for Him.

The disciples who witnessed the conversation between Jesus and this young man understood the cost of following Him. They themselves had left everything to follow Him. After Jesus' conversation with the young man and His comments on treasures in Mark 10, we find this response: *Peter said to him, "We have left everything to follow you!"* (10:28 NIV).

These men understood that following Jesus required sacrifice—a willingness to fully trust Him and surrender anything and everything that might stand in the way of following their King.

PRESENT AND ETERNAL RAMIFICATIONS

It was in response to Peter's statement that Jesus

indicated such sacrifice would be blessed. He responded with the quote that began this chapter:

Truly, I say to you, there is no one who has left house or brothers or sisters or mother or father or children or lands, for my sake and for the gospel, who will not receive a hundredfold now in this time, houses and brothers and sisters and mothers and children and lands, with persecutions, and in the age to come eternal life.

So, just what did Jesus mean with these words? Was He saying that those who sacrificed everything to follow Him would receive deeds to new homes and lands? Would they take on additional biological families? Not quite. But in the King's economy, those who sacrifice to follow Him join an entire community of followers who become family and whose homes and possessions are lovingly and graciously shared with each other as needed.

Back in the Introduction, I mentioned the young men in my discipleship group—every Thursday night, those fifteen guys come to our house and spend the evening in Bible study, prayer, and fellowship. Debbie, my wife, has nine high-school girls at the house every Monday night doing the same thing. They all know that they are family to us—they have become our "kids"—they know that we love them dearly and that our house is truly their home.

Years ago, I was on staff at a church on Long Island, New York. Every Thursday night we had close to forty college and career singles in our home for Bible study. Many of those came from families who were hostile to their faith—for some, to follow Jesus meant that they were cut off completely from their families. But they took on a whole new family—a much larger one with a lot of homes that were opened to them—when they became part of that loving fellowship.

When we follow Jesus, we willingly surrender everything that we are and have over to the King, and surrendering those things can be both painful and frightening. But what we receive in exchange far exceeds anything we could have ever imagined. We are inclined to cling desperately to those things, but they pale in comparison to the glorious blessings He lavishes on us when we release them and follow Him. Surrendering the temporary gratification that comes from earthly possessions and pleasures is a very small price to pay in exchange for the incredible riches of love and fellowship that is shared among those who have given everything over to Him. And that is in addition to the glorious blessing of the loving relationship we have with Him.

But there is also an eternal aspect to all of this. The young man asked what he could do to *inherit eternal life*. Jesus commented about how difficult it was for a rich man to *enter the Kingdom*. The disciples asked *who could be saved*. This passage is not merely addressing the fine points of a "deeper walk" with Jesus, it is addressing salvation. Jesus made it clear that if a person was not willing to surrender everything over to Him, that person had no place in the Kingdom.

That shouldn't surprise us; a person who is not willing to bow before an earthly king would not be welcome in his kingdom—why would we expect it to be different in God's Kingdom? The reality is that the only ones allowed in the Kingdom of Heaven are those who bow before—who recognize and submit to—the King.

> *The reality is that the only ones allowed into the Kingdom of Heaven are those who bow before the King.*

Jesus made the same point in the Matthew passage above. When He indicated that a disciple must deny self, take up his cross, and follow Him, He put it in the context of salvation. Look at the verse again:

If anyone wishes to come after Me, he must deny himself, and take up his cross and follow Me. For whoever wishes to save his life will lose it; but whoever loses his life for My sake will find it. For what will it profit a man if he gains the whole world and forfeits his soul? Or what will a man give in exchange for his soul? (16: 24-26 NASB).

Again, Jesus is not talking about a "deeper walk," He is talking about eternal life. In verse 26, He clearly indicates that the eternal state of a person's soul is at stake. The person who is not willing to deny self, take up the cross, and follow Him—the person who clings to his own life and is not willing to lose it for Him—is forfeiting his soul.

This is **not** to suggest that a person can earn his or her salvation by doing things—we can't, and any hint otherwise leads to the empty ritualism of the rich young ruler. But it does mean that to enter the Kingdom we must acknowledge and humbly bow down before the King, and that means recognizing that all we are and have belongs to Him, not us; the Bible calls this "faith." A person who is not willing to surrender everything and follow Jesus should not be duped into thinking that he or she will spend eternity with Him, regardless of the religious rituals and formulas that person has followed.[1]

Final Thoughts

I remember as a child, back in the days of black and white TVs, watching a *National Geographic* special that showed how local trappers in a village would trap monkeys. It was an incredibly simple and effective device. They would cut a small hole in a coconut and hollow it out, place a piece of fruit inside it, and then attach it by chain to a stake anchored securely in the ground. I watched in amazement as a monkey cautiously approached the coconut, sniffed it, picked it up and inspected it, then inserted its paw through the hole to retrieve the fruit.

But what amazed me more was what happened next. The monkey couldn't pull its paw out of the coconut—it panicked and went berserk. The way it was running and jumping and yanking, I was sure it would either yank the stake out of the ground or tear its arm out of its shoulder socket. I asked my father what happened when the monkey's paw went in the coconut, thinking maybe there was some sort of device inside the coconut that had clamped onto the monkey's paw.

His answer astounded me then and was etched permanently in my mind. He explained that the opening in the coconut was just big enough for the monkey's open paw to squeeze through to grab the fruit, but once he grabbed the fruit inside, the clinched fist was too large to pull back out. He said that all the monkey needed to do was let go of the fruit and it would be free.

But the monkey refused to let go. He clung to that piece of fruit, jumping and flailing wildly as the trappers approached with nets. If he had let go, he could have escaped to freedom, but he refused. The men of the village threw the net over it, and that monkey lived the rest of its life in captivity.

That's exactly what happened to the rich young man. He held tightly to those things that were so alluring, refusing to let go, and in so doing he doomed himself to captivity and bondage—bondage to an unfulfilled and meaningless life, but even more so to the enemy and his devices.

But isn't that what we do? We cling to the things of our lives—money, possessions, aspirations, dreams, control over our own lives, or perhaps even an inappropriate relationship with someone—refusing to see that our grip on those things dooms us to the same bondage the rich young man faced.

The stunning reality is that if we let go—if we will surrender these things to the Lord, if we will relinquish control of our lives to Him—the incomparable and incredibly rich blessings of love and fellowship with Him and His true followers far surpass anything we could ever hope to gain or experience by holding on.

Please allow me to speak on a personal level for a moment. Can you relate to this rich young ruler in some way? Perhaps you have equated righteousness with keeping a strict set of religious rules. If so, you have likely tasted the emptiness that it brings (otherwise, you would not have bought the book and read it to this point). Perhaps you have sought fulfillment in amassing material things or pursuing a position of status so that people look up to you. If that were working for you, again, I don't think you would have read this book.

The absolute reality that we find in this account is that true spiritual fulfillment can never be realized through religious ritual, material possessions, or obtaining status—it can only be found in a Person—The Person—Jesus Christ. And it is not realized by asking Him to follow you around, but rather by surrendering everything over to Him—including your heart—and following Him.

Are you perhaps holding onto something that prevents you from following Jesus? Are you focusing all of your hopes and dreams on that tiny piece of fruit inside the coconut?

Freedom—now and for all eternity—is yours by merely letting go.

---

1. See Blomberg on 16:24-26.

NOTES

GETTING THE MOST FROM GOD

Conclusion

IN THE INTRODUCTION, WE MADE THE point that God *rewards those who earnestly seek him* (Heb. 11:6 NIV). There is no denying that point; but as we have seen in these last four chapters, God does not reward those who earnestly seek *rewards*—He rewards those who earnestly seek *Him*. And ultimately, He *is* the reward—when we seek Him, we are overwhelmed with the incredible riches and blessings of Who He is and of fellowship with Him.

What we've seen in these passages is that the richest blessings in life are directly and inseparably linked to a relationship with Him—a relationship in which we surrender all that we are and all that we have to Him and walk in humble submission to and with Him. Yet, as we surrender and submit to Him in this relationship, He lavishes us with the glorious blessings of His love.

But there is a critical point that we must remember. This relationship was made possible by the sacrificial death of the King. Jesus willingly and lovingly paid the penalty for our sin, a price we could *never* pay, when He gave Himself over to be crucified. Our sin—our insistence on running our own lives, doing things the way we choose, rejecting His authority and disobeying His commands—has separated us from God. It made us His enemies, fully deserving of His wrath, and the price for that sin was blood. Jesus, the High King, had no sin, so He offered His own blood to pay for our sin when He died on the cross; and the great news is that He rose again! And according to God's Word, He graciously and willingly forgives the debt for all who will repent of their sin and trust Him enough to surrender their lives over to the King to follow and serve Him. What an incredible exchange!

So, how does one enter into this relationship? What steps do we take in order to take advantage of the Lord's sacrifice on our behalf?

The Bible gives four commands that are directly linked to entering into this relationship: *repent, believe, call,* and *confess.*

REPENT

When Peter preached to the crowd of people in Jerusalem who had watched him heal a lame man, he proclaimed: *But the things which God announced before-hand by the mouth of all the prophets, that His Christ would suffer, He has thus fulfilled. Therefore* **repent** *and return, so that your sins may be wiped away, in order that times of refreshing may come from the presence of the Lord* (Acts 3:18-19 NASB, emphasis added). The word *repent* means to have a change of heart and mind, which leads to a change of behavior. In the context of his sermon, Peter indicated that the people had rejected Jesus as their Messiah/King. In verse 14, he indicated that they had "disowned the Holy and Righteous One."

> The simple reality is that all of us have rebelled against the King's authority.

His call to the people was to turn back to God, which meant no longer rejecting and rebelling against Him and His Anointed One.

The simple reality is that all of us have rebelled against the King's authority over, and ownership of, our lives and have assumed that position of king over our own lives. Repenting means surrendering that role of king back to Him.

BELIEVE

One of the best known passages in the New Testament is John 3:16: *For God so loved the world, that he gave his only Son, that whoever* **believes** *in him should not perish but have eternal life* (ESV, emphasis added).

The idea of eternal life in this passage is not merely spending eternity in heaven—it is also the quality of life that we inherit when we stop trusting and following our own desires and *believe in*—the Greek word literally means to *trust or have faith in*—Him. And it's not merely believing something about Him—that God gave His Son to die for us. It is believing *in* Jesus—trusting and having faith *in* Him—as God's Son, the Messiah. It literally means entrusting oneself to Him, recognizing and trusting Him for Who He is—our

Master, Lord, and King.

Some may hesitate, thinking they have sinned so much that God could never forgive them. But the Bible says in John 1:12: *But to all who did receive him, who believed in his name, he gave the right to become children of God* (ESV). This means that anyone who receives Him for Who He really is—who trusts in Him as Lord and King—will become His own dear child, regardless of how he has lived or what she has done in the past.

CALL

In Acts 2:21 Peter told the crowd: *And everyone who **calls** on the name of the Lord will be saved* (NIV, emphasis added). This is the point of personal interaction with God when a person actually calls out to God, asking to be delivered from his sin because of Who Jesus is and what He did on the cross. But notice in the passage that it is calling upon the name of the *Lord*. That title for Jesus was synonymous with *king, Messiah,* and *Christ*. It was used to indicate His absolute authority over everyone and everything. It also was used to identify Him as God. Again, it is essential to recognize Him for Who He is—He's not merely the Rescuer, the Deliverer, the

One Who saves us from hell—He is the absolute ruler, the King of the universe Who died for us. And to be saved from our sin and be made right with God requires that we recognize Him for Who He is—our Savior *AND* our Lord.

But again, look at who is welcome to enter into this relationship—*everyone* who calls upon Him. There are no qualifiers based on income, social status, race, sex, appearance, family history, education, IQ, health, weight, accomplishments, awards, or past moral failures. Jesus made it a point to spend time with and show His love to those who were recognized as the most sinful of His day. Because of the cross, He welcomes anyone and everyone who will humbly come to Him as Lord.

Confess

The Apostle Paul said: *If you **confess** with your mouth, "Jesus is Lord," and believe in your heart that God raised him from the dead, you will be saved* (Rom. 10:9 NIV, emphasis added). This decision is personal, but it is not private. While there must be belief in the heart, there must also be corresponding declaration with the mouth. At the same time, while there is declaration from the mouth, there must be corresponding belief in the heart.

The confession affirms our understanding of Who Jesus is, what He has done, and our willingness to recognize and submit to Him as the ultimate and absolute authority in our lives. It is a statement that reflects the decision to no longer look to self as the ruler, but to bow in humble submission before Him.

It also is a statement that reflects the belief of our hearts. When Paul wrote that we must believe that God raised Jesus from the dead, he was not saying we are merely to believe that an event of history actually took place. Jesus' death, burial, and resurrection from the dead was more than a mere point in history or the start of a new religion; it was the crowning achievement of all history in which everything Jesus said about Himself was absolutely validated. Jesus' claims of being the promised Messiah—the Christ, the King, the Son of God—were all confirmed and given ultimate credence on that very first Easter Sunday morning. Our belief in His resurrection is our belief that He was in fact Who He said He was—that singular event justifies and calls for our absolute allegiance to Him.

According to this passage, the Lord expects this internal reality to be reflected in an external affirmation.

This incredible relationship is available to all who will repent and turn to Him because of Who He is and what He has done, trust in Him as Lord, call out to Him to be delivered from sin, and confess Him as Lord.

This does *not* mean you must live a perfect life in order to earn eternal life—that cannot and will not happen. Paul said that being saved from sin is a gift of God and that it is not given based on what we do, but rather is by God's grace and is directly linked to our faith in Him (Eph. 2:8,9).

And it does not mean that you will never stumble. Everyone slips up from time to time. But it does mean that when you disobey you will go to Him for forgiveness (1 John 1:9).

If you have never done this before, are you ready now to follow Him? If so, simply:

Repent—right now determine in your heart and mind that you are turning away from the sin of rejecting God and running your own life, and you are turning to Him and accepting His authority over your life;

Believe—right now decide to entrust your life into His hands;

Call—pray to Him right now. Tell Him you want to trust Him with your life and with your soul. Ask Him to deliver you from your sin—from your rejection of Him and your disobedience—and acknowledge to Him that you realize Jesus died for your sin and that you cannot be right with God apart from His death. Tell Him that you want to surrender your life over to His full authority; and

Confess—tell someone what you have done and why.

Once you have made this decision, there are some follow-up steps that will help you get started in your walk with God. If a friend gave you this book, talk to that friend about your decision. He or she should know of a good church where you can be nurtured and grow. If you found this book on your own, I encourage you to call my friends from the North American Mission Board at 888-Jesus-2008. They will answer any questions you might have and help you with the next step.

A Note to the Skeptic

Perhaps you've gotten to this point and still doubt because you don't accept the historicity or validity of

Jesus as being anything more than a religious teacher. I would encourage you to do some research. If you do, you will find that the historical evidence overwhelmingly supports these facts:

* Jesus claimed to be God in the flesh and He viewed Himself as the fulfillment of all the prophecies of the promised Messiah/King of Israel. As C.S. Lewis pointed out (in so many words), Jesus was either raving mad, the ultimate con man of all time, or Who He actually claimed to be.[1]

* Jesus was actually executed by crucifixion in Jerusalem for claiming to be the Messiah.

* Jesus rose from the dead on the third day following his death. This fact in itself validates and confirms all of the claims of Christ—and it leaves us with the question: "Will I accept Him for Who He claims to be, or will I reject Him in order to maintain control of my life and destiny?"

If you would like to do further research on the evidence, I commend to you *The Case for Christ* by Lee Strobel and *Evidence that Demands a Verdict* by Josh McDowell. These men started out as skeptics, but after doing thorough research and examining the irrefutable evidence, they reached the inescapable conclusion: Jesus actually was Who He claimed to be. They provide much of this evidence in their books.

But I Walked the Aisle and Prayed a Prayer

At some point in your life you may have responded to a pastor's invitation at the end of a church service. You may have gone to the front of the church and prayed with him or a counselor. Does this mean you are saved? Well, the Bible doesn't instruct us to do those things in order to be saved—the New Testament emphasizes the things I've listed above. I know people who

We are not merely saved to heaven, we are saved to walk in a new relationship with Him.

believe that because they went forward at the end of a service and prayed with the pastor they were saved from hell—but that confidence is not well founded.

There are churches all across the country that are filled with people who walked an aisle, prayed a prayer, were baptized, but are on a path to hell when they die.

Again, the question is: "Who's in charge in your

life?" Have you acknowledged His absolute authority over your life, or do you see Jesus' death as merely a means to escape hell? Tragically, some preachers have reduced the death of Christ to merely a premium payment on fire insurance to keep people out of hell. But it is infinitely more—He didn't die merely to save us from hell, He died to save us from our sin. We are not merely saved to heaven, we are saved to walk in a new relationship with Him. And to be delivered from our sin and to this new relationship with him, we must acknowledge Him for Who He is—the absolute Lord of the universe Who died for me, the One Who has every right to rule over my life—and we must bow before Him as such.

If you have never done that, I urge you to do so right now.

A Note to the Believer

You may have already placed your faith in the Lord before reading this book. If so, my prayer is that the Lord has used this book to help put things in perspective and encourage you in your walk. I also hope you will share this book with a friend or family member who has not reached that point. If you do, I have posted some free small-group discussion guides on my website to facilitate Bible studies for those who have not yet placed their faith in Jesus. The address is www.ToKnowGod.org. Would you pray about giving this book to a few unsaved friends, hosting a five-week study, and prayerfully guiding them to a point of decision? All of the study outlines and guidelines are on the site (or will be soon), and they are absolutely free.

I pray the Lord will richly bless you according to these promises as you faithfully seek and follow Him.

---

1. C. S. Lewis, *Mere Christianity.*

NOTES

ABOUT THE AUTHOR

JOHN REVELL is a minister, editor, and author from Nashville, Tennessee. Since 1996, he has served as Associate Editor and Editor of *SBC LIFE*, the official journal of the Southern Baptist Convention's Executive Committee. Prior to that, he served in pastoral ministry for ten years in Long Island, New York, and in South Florida. His articles have been printed, reprinted, and cited in numerous publications, and he has been quoted in such publications as *Newsweek*, *The Los Angeles Times*, and *The Boston Globe*. He is co-author with Ken Connor of **Sinful Silence: When Christians Neglect Their Civic Duty,** also published by Ginosko Publishing.

Also from Ginosko Publishing

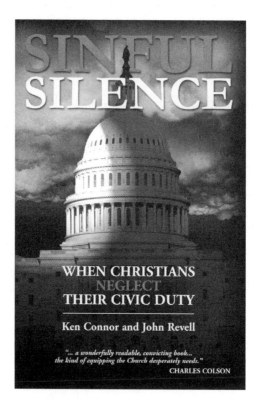

Available at your local bookstore

About Ginosko Publishing

"Gînōskō" (gi-nos-ko) is the Greek verb for "knowing." The concept embodied in the word extends beyond mere intellectual knowledge to include intimate and experiential knowledge.

John Revell has established and embraced the following life goal: "To know and love God and His Word as much as possible, and to help as many as possible do the same." Ginosko Publishing flows out of that goal.

The logo is the Greek letter "Gamma," the first letter in Ginosko, over an open Bible. The products developed and released by Ginosko Publishing have the sole purpose of drawing people into a deeper understanding and appreciation of God's Word, and thereby, a closer relationship with Him.

For more information and helpful resources, go to: www.ToKnowGod.org.

*Now this is eternal life: that they may **know** you, the only true God, and Jesus Christ, whom you have sent.*
(JOHN 17:3)